CLASSICS Illustrated®

William Shakespeare
JULIUS CEASAR

essay by
Julie Bleha, M.A.
Columbia University

ACCLAIM BOOKS
STUDY GUIDE

Julius Caesar

art by Henry Kiefer
cover by Lou Harrison

For Classics Illustrated Study Guides
computer recoloring by Colorgraphix
editor: Madeleine Robins
assistant editor: Gregg Sanderson
design: Scott Friedlander

Classics Illustrated: Julius Caesar © Twin Circle Publishing Co.,
a division of Frawley Enterprises; licensed to First Classics, Inc.
All new material and compilation © 1997 by Acclaim Books, Inc.

Dale-Chall R.L.: 7.3

ISBN 1-57840-038-4

Classics Illustrated® is a registered trademark of the Frawley Corporation.

Acclaim Books, New York, NY
Printed in the United States

STUDY GUIDE

JULIUS CAESAR

BY WILLIAM SHAKESPEARE

CASSIUS

BRUTUS

OCTAVIUS CAESAR

JULIUS CAESAR

S. S.P.Q.R.

CASCA

CINNA

PORTIA

MARK ANTONY

CALPURNIA

IN THE YEAR 44 B.C., JULIUS CAESAR, BRILLIANT ROMAN GENERAL, ORATOR AND STATESMAN, RETURNED TO ROME, VICTORIOUS IN FOREIGN WARS.

THROUGH HIS MILITARY GENIUS, HE HAD CONQUERED MUCH TERRITORY AND ADDED IT TO THE ROMAN EMPIRE; WHILE HIS BRILLIANT ABILITIES AS AN ORATOR AND STATESMAN HAD WON OVER MANY PEOPLE TO HIS AND THE ROMAN STANDARD.

HIS RETURN WAS GREETED WITH WILD ACCLAIM BY ALL ROMANS EXCEPT FOR A FEW CONSPIRATORS WHO, JEALOUS OF HIS POLITICAL STRENGTH AND POPULARITY, WERE CONSPIRING TO BRING ABOUT HIS DOWNFALL. . .

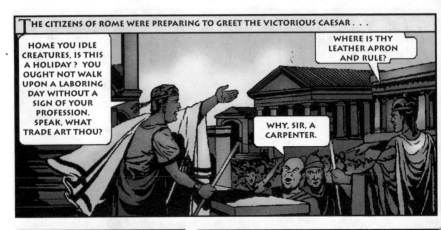

THE CITIZENS OF ROME WERE PREPARING TO GREET THE VICTORIOUS CAESAR...

HOME YOU IDLE CREATURES, IS THIS A HOLIDAY? YOU OUGHT NOT WALK UPON A LABORING DAY WITHOUT A SIGN OF YOUR PROFESSION. SPEAK, WHAT TRADE ART THOU?

WHERE IS THY LEATHER APRON AND RULE?

WHY, SIR, A CARPENTER.

YOU, SIR, WHAT TRADE ART THOU?

A TRADE, SIR, THAT I HOPE I MAY USE WITH A SAFE CONSCIENCE; A MENDER OF BAD SOLES!

WHY DOST THOU LEAD THESE MEN ABOUT THE STREETS?

INDEED, SIR, WE MAKE HOLIDAY TO SEE CAESAR AND TO REJOICE IN HIS TRIUMPH!

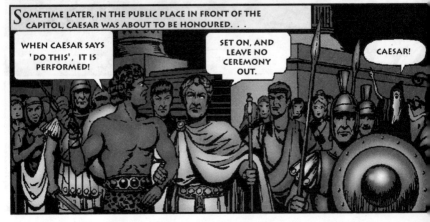

SOMETIME LATER, IN THE PUBLIC PLACE IN FRONT OF THE CAPITOL, CAESAR WAS ABOUT TO BE HONOURED...

WHEN CAESAR SAYS 'DO THIS', IT IS PERFORMED!

SET ON, AND LEAVE NO CEREMONY OUT.

CAESAR!

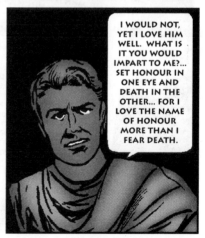

I KNOW THAT VIRTUE TO BE IN YOU, BRUTUS, AS WELL AS I DO KNOW YOUR OUTWARD FAVOUR. WELL, HONOUR IS THE SUBJECT OF MY STORY. I CANNOT TELL WHAT YOU AND OTHER MEN THINK OF THIS LIFE, BUT FOR MY SINGLE SELF, I HAD AS LIEF NOT BE AS LIVE TO BE IN AWE OF SUCH A THING AS I MYSELF. I WAS BORN FREE AS CAESAR; SO WERE YOU: WE BOTH HAVE FED AS WELL, AND WE CAN BOTH ENDURE THE WINTER'S COLD AS WELL AS HE: FOR ONCE, UPON A RAW AND GUSTY DAY, THE TROUBLED TIBER CHAFING WITH HER SHORES, CAESAR SAID TO ME DAREST THOU, CASSIUS, NOW LEAP IN WITH ME INTO THIS ANGRY FLOOD, AND SWIM TO YONDER POINT? UPON THE WORD, ACCOUTRED AS I WAS, I PLUNGED IN AND BADE HIM FOLLOW: SO INDEED HE DID. THE TORRENT ROARED, AND WE DID BUFFET IT WITH LUSTY SINEWS, THROWING IT ASIDE AND STEMMING IT WITH HEARTS OF CONTROVERSY; BUT ERE WE COULD ARRIVE AT THE POINT PROPOSED, CAESAR CRIED 'HELP ME, CASSIUS, OR I SINK!' I, AS AENEAS OUR GREAT ANCESTOR DID FROM THE FLAMES OF TROY UPON HIS SHOULDER THE OLD ANCHISES BEAR, SO FROM THE WAVES OF TIBER DID I THE TIRED CAESAR: AND THIS MAN IS NOW BECOME A GOD, AND CASSIUS IS A WRETCHED CREATURE, AND MUST BEND HIS BODY IF CAESAR CARELESSLY BUT NOD ON HIM. HE HAD A FEVER WHEN HE WAS IN SPAIN, AND WHEN THE FIT WAS ON HIM, I DID MARK HOW HE DID SHAKE: TIS TRUE, THIS GOD DID SHAKE; HIS COWARD LIPS DID FROM THEIR COLOUR FLY, AND THAT SAME EYE WHOSE BEND DOTH AWE THE WORLD DID LOSE HIS LUSTRE... YE GODS! IT DOTH AMAZE ME A MAN OF SUCH FEEBLE TEMPER SHOULD SO GET THE START OF THE MAJESTIC WORLD AND BEAR THE PALM ALONE.

ON THE EVE OF THE IDES OF MARCH . . .

COMES CAESAR TO THE CAPITOL TOMORROW, CASCA ?

HE DOTH. AND NOW FAREWELL, CICERO.

AS CASCA WALKED ALONG, HE WAS SUDDENLY CHALLENGED. . .

WHO'S THERE ?

A ROMAN !

CASCA, BY YOUR VOICE.

YOUR EAR IS GOOD. CASSIUS, WHAT NIGHT IS THIS ?

A VERY PLEASANT NIGHT TO HONEST MEN !

ARE YOU NOT MOVED WHEN ALL THE SWAY OF THE EARTH SHAKES LIKE A THING UNFIRM ? I HAVE SEEN TEMPESTS BUT NEVER TILL TONIGHT DID I GO THROUGH A TEMPEST DROPPING FIRE.

NOW COULD I, CASCA , NAME TO THEE A MAN MOST LIKE THIS DREADFUL NIGHT. A MAN, NO MIGHTIER THAN THYSELF OR ME.

INDEED, THEY SAY THE SENATORS TOMORROW MEAN TO ESTABLISH CAESAR AS KING.

WHY SHOULD CAESAR BE A TYRANT ? HE WOULD NOT BE A WOLF BUT THAT HE SEES THE ROMANS ARE BUT SHEEP.

STAND CLOSE A WHILE FOR HERE COMES ONE IN HASTE.

IT IS CINNA. HE IS A FRIEND. CINNA, WHERE HASTE YOU SO?

TO FIND YOU OUT!

WHO'S THAT?

CASCA. ONE INCORPORATE TO OUR ATTEMPT.

O CASSIUS. IF YOU COULD BUT WIN THE NOBLE BRUTUS TO OUR PARTY!

BE YOU CONTENT. GOOD CINNA, TAKE THIS PAPER AND LAY IT ON THE PRAETOR'S* CHAIR WHERE BRUTUS MAY BUT FIND IT... AND THROW THIS IN AT HIS WINDOW...

*ROMAN JUDGE

COME. CASCA, YOU AND I WILL YET ERE DAY SEE BRUTUS AT HIS HOUSE: THREE PARTS OF HIM IS OURS ALREADY, AND THE NEXT ENCOUNTER YIELDS HIM OURS.

OH! HE SITS HIGH IN ALL THE PEOPLE'S HEARTS, AND THAT WHICH WOULD APPEAR OFFENSE IN US, HIS COUNTENANCE WILL CHANGE TO VIRTUE.

LET US GO. WE WILL WAKE HIM AND BE SURE OF HIM.

MEANWHILE, IN BRUTUS' ORCHARD...

GET ME A TAPER* IN MY STUDY, LUCIUS.

CALLED YOU, MY LORD?

*SMALL CANDLE

THINK YOU, BRUTUS, OF THIS THING. CAESAR WOULD BE CROWNED; HOW THAT MIGHT CHANGE HIS NATURE, THERE'S THE QUESTION! CROWN HIM? THAT? THINK HIM AS A SERPENT'S EGG WHICH HATCHED WOULD GROW MISCHIEVOUS AND KILL HIM IN THE SHELL.

IS NOT TOMORROW, BOY, THE IDES OF MARCH? LOOK IN THE CALENDAR AND BRING ME WORD.

THE TAPER BURNETH IN YOUR CLOSET, SIR. SEARCHING THE WINDOW FOR A FLINT, I FOUND THIS PAPER.

MY ANCESTORS DID, FROM THE STREETS OF ROME, THE TARQUIN DRIVE WHEN HE WAS CALLED A KING. AM I ENTREATED TO SPEAK AND STRIKE?... SOMEONE KNOCKS!

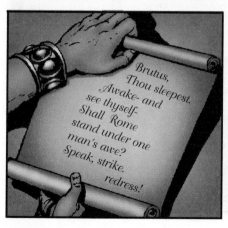

Brutus,
Thou sleepest.
Awake- and
see thyself-
Shall Rome
stand under one
man's awe?
Speak, strike,
redress!

SIR, 'TIS YOUR BROTHER, CASSIUS, AT THE DOOR, THERE ARE MORE WITH HIM.

LET THEM ENTER.

I THINK WE ARE TOO BOLD UPON YOUR REST. GOOD MORROW, BRUTUS, DO WE TROUBLE YOU?

I HAVE BEEN UP THIS HOUR, AWAKE ALL NIGHT.

SHALL I ENTREAT A WORD?

THERE LIES THE EAST. DOTH NOT THE DAY BREAK THERE?

IT DOTH, AND YON GREY LINES ARE MESSENGERS OF DAY.

NOW, LET US SWEAR OUR RESOLUTION.

NO, NOT AN OATH. WHAT OTHER BOND NEED WE THAN SECRET ROMANS THAT HAVE SPOKEN THE WORD? GIVE ME YOUR HANDS, ALL OVER, ONE BY ONE.

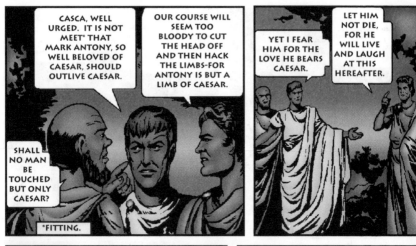

PORTIA LEFT AS LUCIUS ENTERED WITH AN OLD MAN...

LUCIUS, WHO'S THAT KNOCKS?

HERE IS A SICK MAN THAT WOULD SPEAK WITH YOU.

VOUCH SAFE GOOD MORROW FROM A FEEBLE TONGUE.

CAIUS LIGARIUS. O, WOULD YOU WERE NOT SICK.

I AM NOT SICK IF BRUTUS HAVE IN HAND ANY EXPLOIT WORTHY THE NAME OF HONOUR.

SUCH AN EXPLOIT HAVE I IN HAND, LIGARIUS, HAD YOU A HEALTHFUL EAR TO HEAR IT.

BY ALL THE GODS THAT ROMANS BOW BEFORE, I NOW DISCARD MY SICKNESS. WHATS'S TO DO?

A PIECE OF WORK THAT WILL MAKE SICK MEN WHOLE.

THE IDES OF MARCH . . . ABOUT THE EIGHTH HOUR . . . IN CAESAR'S HOUSE . . .

NOR HEAVEN NOR EARTH HAVE BEEN AT PEACE TONIGHT. THRICE HATH MY CALPURNIA IN HER SLEEP CRIED OUT. "HELP, HO, THEY MURDER CAESAR!"

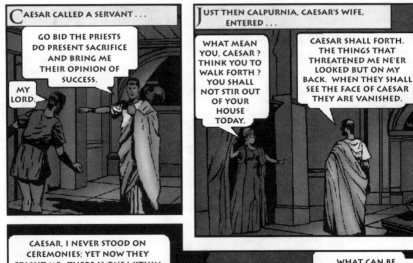

CAESAR CALLED A SERVANT...

GO BID THE PRIESTS DO PRESENT SACRIFICE AND BRING ME THEIR OPINION OF SUCCESS.

MY LORD.

JUST THEN CALPURNIA, CAESAR'S WIFE, ENTERED...

WHAT MEAN YOU, CAESAR? THINK YOU TO WALK FORTH? YOU SHALL NOT STIR OUT OF YOUR HOUSE TODAY.

CAESAR SHALL FORTH. THE THINGS THAT THREATENED ME NE'ER LOOKED BUT ON MY BACK. WHEN THEY SHALL SEE THE FACE OF CAESAR THEY ARE VANISHED.

CAESAR, I NEVER STOOD ON CEREMONIES; YET NOW THEY FRIGHT ME. THERE IS ONE WITHIN RECOUNTS HORRID SIGHTS SEEN BY THE WATCH. THAT GRAVES HAVE YAWNED AND YIELDED UP THEIR DEAD, AND GHOSTS DID SHRIEK AND SQUEAL ABOUT THE STREETS. O, CAESAR, THESE THINGS ARE BEYOND ALL USE AND I DO FEAR THEM.

WHAT CAN BE AVOIDED WHOSE END IS PURPOS'D BY THE MIGHTY GODS? AND THESE PREDICTIONS ARE TO THE WORLD IN GENERAL AS TO CAESAR.

THE SERVANT RETURNED FROM THE TEMPLE...

WHAT SAY THE AUGERERS?*

THEY WOULD NOT HAVE YOU STIR FORTH TODAY. PLUCKING THE ENTRAILS OF AN OFFERING, THEY COULD NOT FIND A HEART WITHIN THE BEAST.

*ROMAN PROPHETS

THE GODS DO THIS IN SHAME OF COWARDICE. CAESAR SHOULD BE A BEAST IF HE STAY HOME TODAY.

ALAS, MY LORD, YOUR WISDOM IS CONSUMED IN CONFIDENCE.

WE'LL SEND MARK ANTONY TO THE SENATE TO SAY YOU ARE NOT WELL TODAY.

FOR YOUR HUMOUR, I WILL STAY AT HOME. ...HERE'S DECIUS; HE SHALL TELL THEM.

GOOD MORROW, WORTHY CAESAR.

YOU COME JUST IN TIME TO BEAR MY GREETINGS TO THE SENATORS AND TELL THEM I WILL NOT COME TODAY.

MOST MIGHTY CAESAR, LET ME KNOW SOME CAUSE.

SAY HE IS SICK.

HAVE I IN CONQUEST STRETCHED MINE ARM SO FAR TO BE AFEARED TO TELL GREYBEARDS THE TRUTH ? THE CAUSE IS IN MY WILL; THAT IS ENOUGH TO SATISFY THE SENATE.

THE SENATE HAVE CONCLUDED TO GIVE THIS DAY A CROWN TO MIGHTY CAESAR. IF YOU SHALL SEND THEM WORD YOU WILL NOT COME, THEIR MINDS MAY CHANGE. IF CAESAR HIDE HIMSELF, SHALL NOT THEY WHISPER "LO, CAESAR IS AFRAID !" ?

HOW FOOLISH YOUR FEARS SEEM NOW, CALPURNIA. GIVE ME MY ROBE, FOR I WILL GO.

GOOD MORROW, CAESAR.

MEANWHILE, NEAR THE STEPS OF THE CAPITOL...

HERE WILL I STAND TILL CAESAR PASS ALONG, AND I WILL GIVE HIM THIS.

IF THOU READ THIS, O. CAESAR, THOU MAY'ST LIVE. IF NOT, THE FATES WITH TRAITORS DO CONTRIVE. BUT HERE COMES CAESAR NOW!

Caesar, beware of Brutus, Cassius, Casca, Cinna and Ligarius. There is but one mind in all these men and it is bent against Caesar. If thou be not immortal, Look about you; security gives way to conspiracy. The mighty Gods defend thee! Thy Lover, Artemidorus.

AT THE STEPS OF THE CAPITOL, CAESAR SAW THE OLD SOOTHSAYER WHO HAD WARNED HIM TO "BEWARE THE IDES OF MARCH..."

THE IDES OF MARCH ART COME.

AYE, BUT NOT GONE.

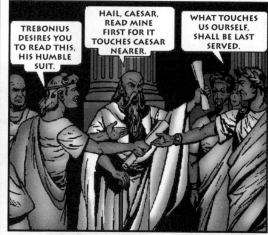

TREBONIUS DESIRES YOU TO READ THIS, HIS HUMBLE SUIT.

HAIL, CAESAR, READ MINE FIRST FOR IT TOUCHES CAESAR NEARER.

WHAT TOUCHES US OURSELF, SHALL BE LAST SERVED.

DELAY NOT, CAESAR! READ IT INSTANTLY!

SIRRAH, GIVE PLACE!

WHAT! IS THE FELLOW MAD?

AS CAESAR AND THE OTHERS PROCEEDED UP THE CAPITOL STEPS...

I WISH YOUR ENTERPRISE TODAY MAY THRIVE, CASSIUS.

WHAT ENTERPRISE, POPILIUS?

FARE YOU WELL.

HE WISHED TODAY OUR ENTERPRISE MIGHT THRIVE. I FEAR OUR PURPOSE IS DISCOVERED.

TREBONIUS KNOWS HIS TIME; FOR LOOK YOU, BRUTUS, HE DRAWS MARK ANTONY OUT OF THE WAY.

CASCA, YOU ARE THE FIRST THAT REARS YOUR HAND.

WHAT IS NOW AMISS THAT CAESAR AND HIS SENATE MUST REDRESS?

MOST MIGHTY CAESAR, METELLUS CIMBER THROWS BEFORE THY SEAT A HUMBLE HEART...

I MUST PREVENT THEE, CIMBER. THY BROTHER BY DECREE IS BANISHED.

I KISS THY HAND, BUT NOT IN FLATTERY, CAESAR, DESIRING THEE THAT PUBLIUS CIMBER MAY HAVE AN IMMEDIATE FREEDOM OF REPEAL.

WHAT, BRUTUS!

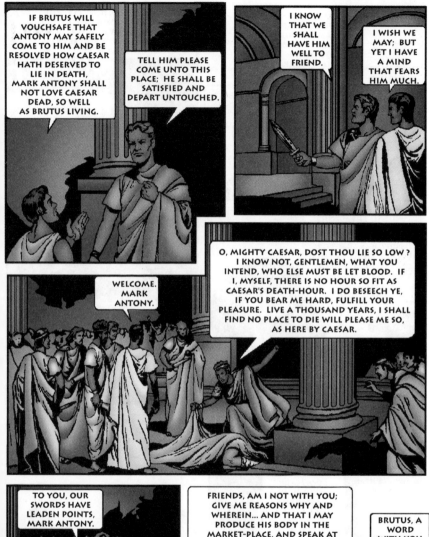

DO NOT CONSENT THAT ANTONY SHOULD SPEAK.

MARK ANTONY, YOU SHALL NOT IN YOUR FUNERAL SPEECH BLAME US BUT SPEAK ALL GOOD YOU CAN OF CAESAR. YOU SHALL SPEAK AFTER MY SPEECH IS ENDED.

BE IT SO.

THEN ALL BUT ANTONY LEFT THE SENATE. ANTONY WAS INSTRUCTED TO PREPARE THE BODY AND FOLLOW THEM TO THE PUBLIC PLACE WHERE CAESAR'S FUNERAL WAS TO BE HELD...

OH, PARDON ME, THOU BLEEDING PIECE OF EARTH, THAT I AM MEEK AND GENTLE WITH THESE BUTCHERS!

WOE TO THE HAND THAT SHED THIS COSTLY BLOOD, FOR CAESAR'S SPIRIT, RANGING FOR REVENGE, SHALL IN THESE CONFINES CRY HAVOC! THIS FOUL DEED SHALL SMELL ABOVE THE EARTH.

POST BACK WITH SPEED AND TELL YOUR MASTER WHAT HATH CHANCED.

A SERVANT ENTERED...

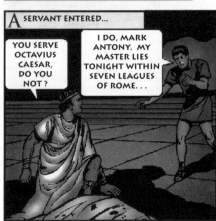

YOU SERVE OCTAVIUS CAESAR, DO YOU NOT?

I DO, MARK ANTONY. MY MASTER LIES TONIGHT WITHIN SEVEN LEAGUES OF ROME...

IN THE PUBLIC PLACE, BRUTUS ADDRESSED THE ROMAN CITIZENS WHO WERE CLAMORING FOR REASONS FOR CAESAR'S MURDER...

GIVE ME AUDIENCE, FRIENDS. PUBLIC REASON SHALL BE RENDERED OF CAESAR'S DEATH.

I WILL HEAR BRUTUS SPEAK.

THE NOBLE BRUTUS! SILENCE!

ROMANS, COUNTRYMEN... IF THERE BE IN THIS ASSEMBLY ANY DEAR FRIEND OF CAESAR'S, TO HIM I SAY THAT BRUTUS' LOVE TO CAESAR WAS NO LESS THAN HIS. IF THAT FRIEND THEN DEMAND WHY BRUTUS ROSE AGAINST CAESAR, THIS IS MY ANSWER... NOT THAT I LOVED CAESAR LESS, BUT THAT I LOVED ROME MORE. AS CAESAR WAS VALIANT, I HONOURED HIM. AS HE WAS AMBITIOUS, I SLEW HIM. HAD YOU RATHER CAESAR WERE LIVING, AND DIE ALL SLAVES, THAN CAESAR WERE DEAD, TO LIVE ALL FREE MEN? WHO HERE IS SO BASE THAT WOULD BE A BONDMAN, SO RUDE THAT WOULD NOT BE A ROMAN, SO VILE THAT WOULD NOT LOVE HIS COUNTRY? IF ANY, SPEAK FOR HIM I HAVE OFFENDED.

NONE, BRUTUS, NONE!

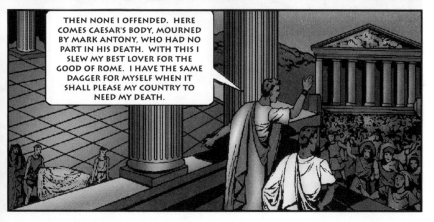

THEN NONE I OFFENDED. HERE COMES CAESAR'S BODY, MOURNED BY MARK ANTONY, WHO HAD NO PART IN HIS DEATH. WITH THIS I SLEW MY BEST LOVER FOR THE GOOD OF ROME. I HAVE THE SAME DAGGER FOR MYSELF WHEN IT SHALL PLEASE MY COUNTRY TO NEED MY DEATH.

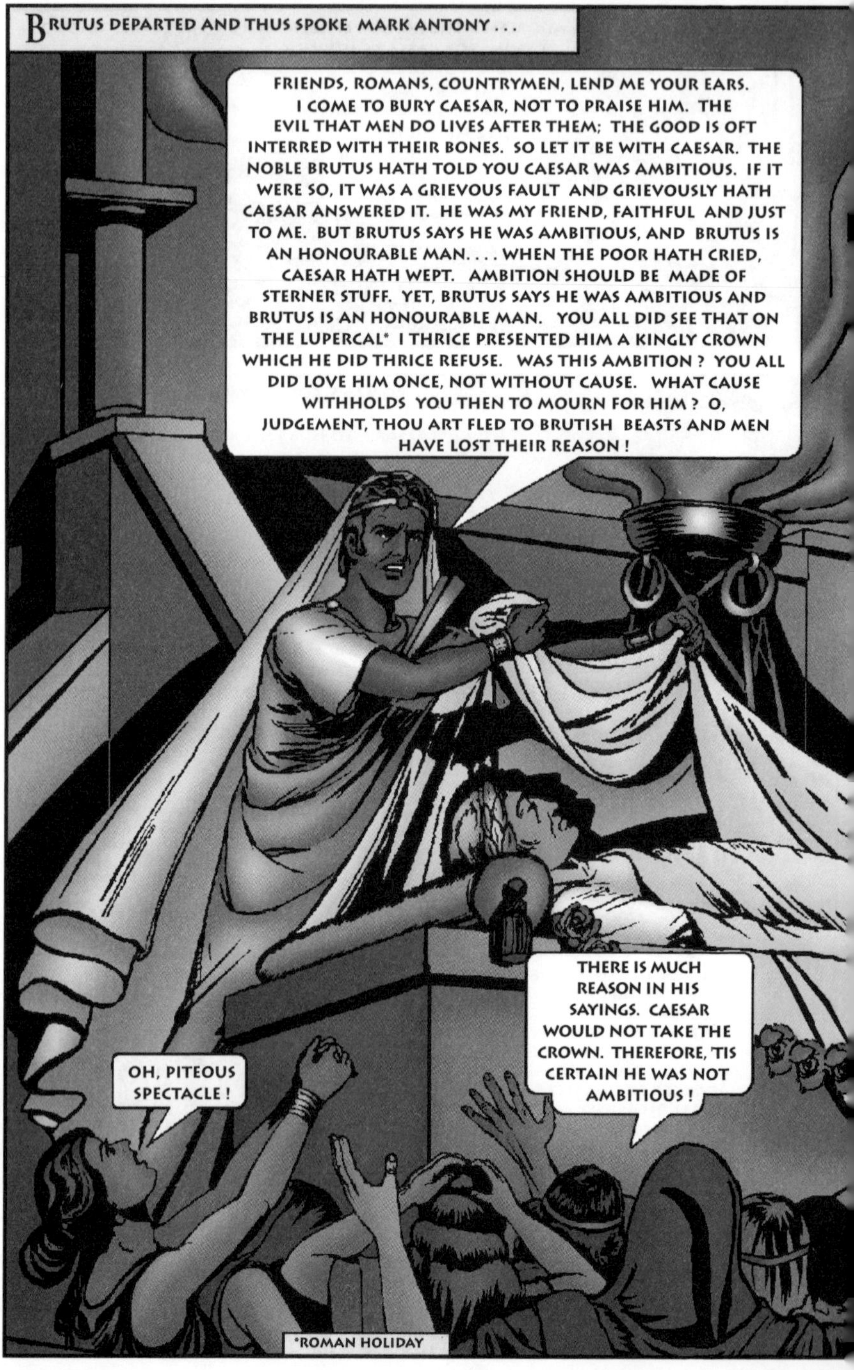
BRUTUS DEPARTED AND THUS SPOKE MARK ANTONY . . .
FRIENDS, ROMANS, COUNTRYMEN, LEND ME YOUR EARS. I COME TO BURY CAESAR, NOT TO PRAISE HIM. THE EVIL THAT MEN DO LIVES AFTER THEM; THE GOOD IS OFT INTERRED WITH THEIR BONES. SO LET IT BE WITH CAESAR. THE NOBLE BRUTUS HATH TOLD YOU CAESAR WAS AMBITIOUS. IF IT WERE SO, IT WAS A GRIEVOUS FAULT AND GRIEVOUSLY HATH CAESAR ANSWERED IT. HE WAS MY FRIEND, FAITHFUL AND JUST TO ME. BUT BRUTUS SAYS HE WAS AMBITIOUS, AND BRUTUS IS AN HONOURABLE MAN. . . . WHEN THE POOR HATH CRIED, CAESAR HATH WEPT. AMBITION SHOULD BE MADE OF STERNER STUFF. YET, BRUTUS SAYS HE WAS AMBITIOUS AND BRUTUS IS AN HONOURABLE MAN. YOU ALL DID SEE THAT ON THE LUPERCAL* I THRICE PRESENTED HIM A KINGLY CROWN WHICH HE DID THRICE REFUSE. WAS THIS AMBITION ? YOU ALL DID LOVE HIM ONCE, NOT WITHOUT CAUSE. WHAT CAUSE WITHHOLDS YOU THEN TO MOURN FOR HIM ? O, JUDGEMENT, THOU ART FLED TO BRUTISH BEASTS AND MEN HAVE LOST THEIR REASON !
THERE IS MUCH REASON IN HIS SAYINGS. CAESAR WOULD NOT TAKE THE CROWN. THEREFORE, 'TIS CERTAIN HE WAS NOT AMBITIOUS !
OH, PITEOUS SPECTACLE !
*ROMAN HOLIDAY

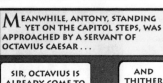

MEANWHILE, ANTONY, STANDING YET ON THE CAPITOL STEPS, WAS APPROACHED BY A SERVANT OF OCTAVIUS CAESAR . . .

SIR, OCTAVIUS IS ALREADY COME TO ROME. HE AND LEPIDUS ARE AT CAESAR'S HOUSE.

AND THITHER I WILL STRAIGHT TO VISIT HIM.

I HEARD HIM SAY BRUTUS AND CASSIUS ARE RID LIKE MADMEN THROUGH THE GATES OF ROME. BELIKE THEY HAD SOME NOTICE OF THE PEOPLE . . HOW YOU HAD MOV'D THEM.

FORTUNE IS MERRY AND IN THIS MOOD WILL GIVE US ANYTHING.

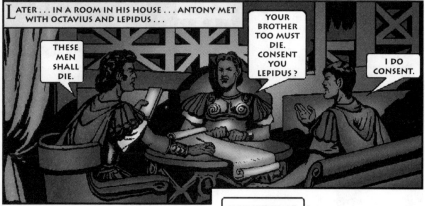

LATER . . . IN A ROOM IN HIS HOUSE . . . ANTONY MET WITH OCTAVIUS AND LEPIDUS . . .

THESE MEN SHALL DIE.

YOUR BROTHER TOO MUST DIE. CONSENT YOU LEPIDUS ?

I DO CONSENT.

UPON CONDITION PUBLIUS SHALL NOT LIVE, WHO IS YOUR SISTER'S SON, ANTONY. . .

HE SHALL NOT LIVE. LOOK WITH A SPOT I DAMN HIM.

BUT LEPIDUS, GO FETCH CAESAR'S WILL HITHER.

SHALL I FIND YOU HERE ?

. . . OR AT THE CAPITOL.

THIS IS A SLIGHT, UNMERITABLE MAN. IT IS FIT, THE THREEFOLD WORLD DIVIDED, HE SHOULD STAND ONE OF THE THREE TO SHARE IT?

SO YOU THOUGHT HIM! AND TOOK HIS VOICE WHO SHOULD BE PICKED TO DIE!

THOUGH WE LAY THESE HONOURS ON THIS MAN HE SHALL BUT BEAR THEM AS THE MULE BEARS GOLD... TO GROAN AND SWEAT UNDER.

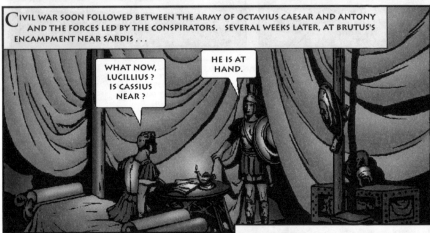

CIVIL WAR SOON FOLLOWED BETWEEN THE ARMY OF OCTAVIUS CAESAR AND ANTONY AND THE FORCES LED BY THE CONSPIRATORS. SEVERAL WEEKS LATER, AT BRUTUS'S ENCAMPMENT NEAR SARDIS...

WHAT NOW, LUCILLIUS? IS CASSIUS NEAR?

HE IS AT HAND.

WITH COURTESY AND RESPECT ENOUGH, BUT NOT WITH SUCH FREE AND FRIENDLY CONFERENCE AS HE HATH USED OF OLD.

A WORD, LUCILLIUS; HOW HE RECEIVED, YOU LET ME BE RESOLVED.

THEY MEAN THIS NIGHT IN SARDIS TO BE QUARTERED.. HARK, HE IS ARRIVED.

THOU HAST DESCRIBED A HOT FRIEND COOLING. THERE ARE NO TRICKS IN PLAIN AND SIMPLE FAITH. COMES HIS ARMY ON?

CASSIUS ENTERED THE TENT . . .

MOST NOBLE BROTHER, YOU HAVE DONE ME WRONG.

JUDGE ME, YOU GODS! WRONG I MINE ENEMIES? AND IF NOT SO, HOW SHOULD I WRONG A BROTHER?

YOU HAVE CONDEMNED LUCIUS PELLA FOR TAKING BRIBES. WHEREIN MY LETTERS PRAYING ON HIS SIDE WERE SLIGHTED OFF.

YOU WRONGED YOURSELF TO WRITE IN SUCH A CASE.

LET ME TELL YOU, CASSIUS, YOU YOURSELF ARE MUCH CONDEMNED TO HAVE AN ITCHING PALM, TO SELL YOUR OFFICES FOR GOLD.

I AN ITCHING PALM? . . . BRUTUS, BAIT NOT ME. I'LL NOT ENDURE IT. I AM A SOLDIER, I, OLDER IN PRACTICE, ABLER THAN YOURSELF.

AWAY, SLIGHT MAN! YOU SAY YOU ARE A BETTER SOLDIER, LET IT APPEAR SO.

MESSALA, ONE OF BRUTUS' GENERALS, ENTERED AS THEY SPOKE...

SPEAK NO MORE OF HER... GIVE ME A BOWL OF WINE... WELCOME GOOD MESSALA.

MESSALA, I HAVE RECIEVED LETTERS THAT YOUNG OCTAVIUS AND MARK ANTONY COME DOWN UPON US WITH A MIGHTY POWER, BENDING THEIR EXPEDITON TOWARDS PHILIPPI * WHAT DO YOU THINK OF MARCHING TO PHILLIPI PRESENTLY ?

I DO NOT THINK IT IS GOOD. 'TIS BETTER THAT THE ENEMY SEEK US !

* PLAINS IN NORTHERN GREECE

THE PEOPLE 'TWIXT PHILIPPI AND THIS GROUND DO STAND IN A FORCED AFFECTION, THEY HAVE GRUDGED US CONTRIBUTION. THE ENEMY INCREASETH EVERY DAY ... WE AT THE HEIGHT, ARE READY TO DECLINE. THERE IS A TIDE IN THE AFFAIRS OF MEN, WHICH TAKEN AT FLOOD LEADS TO FORTUNE. OMITTED, ALL THE VOYAGE OF THEIR LIFE IS BOUND IN SHALLOWS AND MISERIES ...

ON SUCH A SEA ARE WE NOW AFLOAT, AND WE MUST TAKE THE CURRENT WHEN IT SERVES OR LOSE OUR VENTURES.

THEN, WITH YOUR WILL, GO ON. WE'LL ALONG OURSELVES AND MEET THEM AT PHILIPPI.

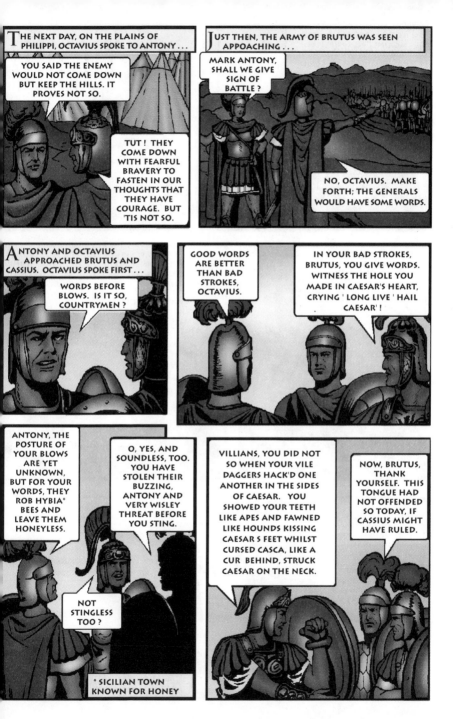

LOOK. I DRAW A SWORD AGAINST CONSPIRITORS. WHEN THINK YOU THAT THIS SWORD GOES UP AGAIN? NEVER, TILL CAESAR'S THREE AND THIRTY WOUNDS BE WELL AVENGED.

COME, ANTONY, AWAY. DEFIANCE, TRAITORS, HURL WE IN YOUR TEETH.

WHEN ANTONY AND OCTAVIUS HAD GONE, CASSIUS SPOKE THUS . . .

WHY, NOW THE STORM IS UP AND ALL IS ON THE HAZARD. I AM COMPELLED TO SET UPON ONE BATTLE ALL OUR LIBERTIES.

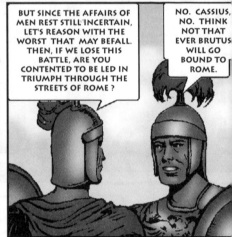

BUT SINCE THE AFFAIRS OF MEN REST STILL INCERTAIN, LET'S REASON WITH THE WORST THAT MAY BEFALL. THEN, IF WE LOSE THIS BATTLE, ARE YOU CONTENTED TO BE LED IN TRIUMPH THROUGH THE STREETS OF ROME?

NO. CASSIUS, NO. THINK NOT THAT EVER BRUTUS WILL GO BOUND TO ROME.

BUT THIS SAME DAY MUST END THE WORK THE IDES OF MARCH BEGUN; AND WHETHER WE SHALL MEET AGAIN I KNOW NOT. THEREFORE OUR EVERLASTING FAREWELL TAKE.

FOREVER AND FOREVER FAREWELL, BRUTUS. IF WE DO MEET AGAIN, WE'LL SMILE INDEED. IF NOT, 'TIS TRUE THIS PARTING WAS WELL MADE.

O, THAT A MAN MIGHT KNOW THE END OF THIS DAY'S BUSINESS ERE IT COMES!... COME, HO! AWAY!

THE TWO ARMIES FACED EACH OTHER AND THE FATE OF THE ROMAN WORLD HUNG IN THE BALANCE...

SOON, THE INFANTRY MET IN VICIOUS HAND TO HAND COMBAT...

BUT ANTONY'S FORCE OF MOUNTED WARRIORS PROVED TO BE DECISIVE...

BRUTUS VIEWED THE BATTLE FROM A HILL-TOP.

MESSALA, I PERCEIVE BUT COLD DEMEANOUR IN OCTAVIUS' WING. RIDE, RIDE AND GIVE THESE BILLS UNTO THE LEGIONS ON THE OTHER SIDE. LET THEM ALL COME DOWN.

ANOTHER PART OF THE FIELD . . . TITINIUS AND CASSIUS WATCHED THE BATTLE IN DESPAIR . . .

OH, CASSIUS, BRUTUS GAVE THE WORD TOO EARLY. HIS SOLDIERS FELL TO SPOIL, WHILE WE, BY ANTONY ARE ALL ENCLOS'D.

RUSHING TO CASSIUS, TITINIUS URGED CASSIUS TO FLEE FOR HIS LIFE . . .

CASSIUS, FLY. WE ARE SURROUNDED ALL ABOUT BY ANTONY.

SOON ANTONY AND HIS MEN ARRIVE AT CASSIUS' CAMP . . .

THE CAMP OF CASSIUS ! SET YOUR TORCH TO IT !

THIS HILL IS FAR ENOUGH . . . TITINIUS, ARE THOSE MY TENTS WHERE I PERCEIVE THE FIRE?

THEY ARE, MY LORD.

TITINIUS, MOUNT AND SPUR TO YONDER TROOPS THAT I MAY REST ASSUR'D WHETHER YOND TROOPS ARE FRIEND OR ENEMY.

GO, PINDARUS, GET HIGHER ON THAT HILL. REGARD TITINIUS, AND TELL ME WHAT THOU NOTEST ABOUT THE FIELD.

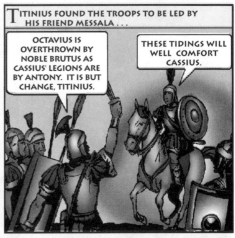

TITINIUS FOUND THE TROOPS TO BE LED BY HIS FRIEND MESSALA . . .

OCTAVIUS IS OVERTHROWN BY NOBLE BRUTUS AS CASSIUS' LEGIONS ARE BY ANTONY. IT IS BUT CHANGE, TITINIUS.

THESE TIDINGS WILL WELL COMFORT CASSIUS.

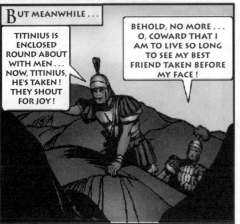

BUT MEANWHILE . . .

TITINIUS IS ENCLOSED ROUND ABOUT WITH MEN . . . NOW, TITINIUS, HE'S TAKEN! THEY SHOUT FOR JOY!

BEHOLD, NO MORE . . . O, COWARD THAT I AM TO LIVE SO LONG TO SEE MY BEST FRIEND TAKEN BEFORE MY FACE!

MY LIFE IS RUN HIS COMPASS. I SWORE THEE, SAVING OF THY LIFE IN PARTHIA, THAT WHATSOEVER I BID THEE DO THOU SHOULD ATTEMPT IT. TAKE THIS GOOD SWORD, THAT RAN THROUGH CAESAR AND SEARCH THIS BOSOM.

GUIDE THOU THE SWORD.

COME, LET US TO THE FIELD AND SET OUR BATTLES ON. 'TIS THREE O'CLOCK AND ROMANS, YET ERE NIGHT, WE SHALL TRY FORTUNE IN A SECOND FIGHT!

LATER THAT AFTERNOON, ON THE BATTLEFIELD. BRUTUS MADE AN APPEAL TO HIS TIRED SOLDIERS . . .

OH, COUNTRYMEN, HOLD UP YOUR HEADS!

ONE OF BRUTUS' YOUNG GENERALS SPEARHEADED THE LAST DESPERATE ATTACK . . .

I AM THE SON OF MARCUS CATO, HO! A FOE TO TYRANTS AND MY COUNTRY'S FRIEND!

CATO SPRANG UPON THE ENEMY, BUT QUICKLY RECIEVED A MORTAL BLOW . . .

LUCIUS, BRUTUS' SERVANT KNELT AT CATO'S BODY...

O CATO, WHY NOW THOU DIEST AS BRAVLEY AS DID TITINIUS.

YIELD, OR THOU DIEST.

ONLY I YIELD TO DIE. KILL BRUTUS AND BE HONOURED IN HIS DEATH.

WE MUST NOT... A NOBLE PRISONER.

TELL ANTONY... BRUTUS IS TA'EN!

HERE COMES THE GENERAL. BRUTUS IS TA'EN MY LORD.

WHERE IS HE?

BRUTUS IS SAFE ENOUGH. I DARE ASSURE THEE THAT NO ENEMY SHALL TAKE ALIVE THE NOBLE BRUTUS.

THIS IS NOT BRUTUS, FRIEND. KEEP THIS MAN SAFE. GIVE HIM ALL KINDNESS. I HAD RATHER HAD SUCH MEN MY FRIEND THAN ENEMIES. GO ON AND SEE WHETHER BRUTUS BE ALIVE OR DEAD.

MEANWHILE, IN ANOTHER PART OF THE FIELD, BRUTUS STOPPED TO REST...

COME, FRIENDS. REST ON THIS ROCK. COME HITHER, CLITUS, LIST A WORD...

WHAT SAYS MY LORD?

WHY, THIS, THE GHOST OF CAESAR HATH APPEARED TO ME TWO TIMES BY NIGHT . . . I KNOW MY HOUR IS COME.

NOT SO MY LORD.

NAY, I AM SURE OF IT. OUR ENEMIES HAVE BEAT US TO THE PIT. HOLD THOU MY SWORDHILTS WHILST I RUN ON IT.

THAT'S NOT THE OFFICE FOR A FRIEND. FLY, FLY, MY LORD. THERE IS NO TARRYING HERE.

FAREWELL TO YOU, COUNTRYMEN, MY HEART DOTH JOY THAT YET IN ALL MY LIFE I FOUND NO MAN BUT HE WAS TRUE TO ME. I SHALL HAVE GLORY BY LOSING THIS DAY.

FLY, MY LORD, FLY !

HENCE I WILL FOLLOW !

I PRITHEE, STATO, STAY THOU BY THY LORD. THOU ART A FELLOW OF GOOD RESPECT. HOLD THEN MY SWORD AND TURN AWAY THY FACE WHILE I DO RUN UPON IT.

GIVE ME YOUR HAND FIRST. FAREWELL MY LORD.

JULIUS CAESAR
WILLIAM SHAKESPEARE

The Author

The Elizabethan Age—William Shakespeare's era in English history—is a link between the Middle Ages and what we call the Modern Era. There were tremendous changes and advances in all aspects of English life, including science, religion, art and politics; centuries-old habits of commerce and agriculture were undergoing similar changes. England was undergoing a Renaissance, and as in all times of social and economic upheaval, the fortunes of some previously humble families rose quickly, while fortunes tumbled downwards for those who had made a steady (but by no means luxurious) living off of the land.

In this time of change, men such as William Shakespeare's father John saw the opportunity to climb the economic, and hence the social, ladder far more quickly than had been possible in earlier times. The elder Shakespeare seized his opportunities—including marriage with Mary Arden, the daughter of a wealthy farmer—and in his lifetime went from simple merchant and glovemaker to *gentle-man* (that is, a person who had the right to have a coat of arms which displayed the family name). William was born (in 1564) and raised in the market town of Stratford-upon-Avon, in England's West Country.

As the son of an up-and-coming town merchant, William would have attended the village grammar school. In this school, and in the "petty school" which was the first educational stop for boys (girls were generally excluded from any kind of intensive education) students learned to read and write not only English, but Latin and Greek. Elizabethans enormously admired the art and culture of ancient Greece and Rome, and these arts, and languages, were considered staples of a good "classical" education. Rhetoric—the art of persuasion—would have been part the young William's education, and in *Julius Caesar* you can see Shakespeare make use of this training, using rhetorical speech as a dramatic tool. Some critics have doubted that a boy from a middle-class background could have grown up to be the man who authored Shakespeare's works. This claim betrays some subtle

class prejudices on the part of the accusers, implying that only a member of the nobility would have been well-read enough to have written the plays; it disallows William's education at Stratford's grammar school.

In 1582, Shakespeare married Anne Hathaway, and the next year their first child, daughter Susanna, was born. Twins, a boy named Hamnet and a girl named Judith, were born two years later. Shakespeare was in London by 1592, and was beginning to make a name for himself as a playwright, though the few years before he came to London are unaccounted for in historical record; it's thought that he worked as an actor with traveling theater companies.

He stayed in London for about twenty years, becoming more and more successful in his work as an actor, writer, and shareholder in his acting company. He then retired to Stratford to lead the life of a country gentleman. Shakespeare died there—on what is thought to be his birthday—in 1616. He is buried in the parish church, where his grave can be seen to this day.

Shakespeare's Stage

As with many other aspects of Elizabethan life, the theater in late 16th-century England saw a flurry of activity and growth. There had always been a strong tradition of theater, as evidenced by the many companies which traveled all across the kingdom. These companies performed in the courtyards of public inns or at street fairs. (In fact, it was the design of these innyards which gave rise to the designs for the first professional theater spaces.) Two important shifts occurred during Shakespeare's youth: first, the theater became profitable enough that purpose-built theatres were going up outside of London's city walls (in areas known as "the liberties," because they weren't subject to strict licensing laws—which is why we

Vagabonds, Sturdy Beggars and Players

When economic and agricultural changes in life in the Elizabethan era resulted in (among other things) a new class of landless people, the English Parliament made an attempt to control this group, passing a stream of edicts which were meant to regulate "vagabonds" (homeless people) and their like. Reading these laws, it sounds like a state of anarchy existed; it was said that the whole land was "presently with rogues, vagabonds and sturdy beggars exceedingly pestered, by means whereof daily happeneth horrible murders, thefts and other great outrages." In 1573, the year after that law was passed, the term "vagabond" came to include all players and minstrels not under the employment of a great lord—in other words, most such people in England!

also find note of bordellos, beer-gardens, and bear-baiting in these neighborhoods). Secondly, members of the nobility became interested in the burgeoning theatre, and several of them took under their "protection" whole companies; hence, troupes were given names such as the Lord Chamberlain's Men (Shakespeare's own company). The profession was coming to be seen as (slightly) more respectable. This combination of profitability and emerging respectability jump-started the life of the English theater—just in time for the arrival in London of young Will Shakespeare.

Today, most stages are proscenium stages; this means that the stage is set back behind a "frame;" the bigger the house seating area, the further the distance between most of the audience and the stage, actors, and action. By comparison, the theaters of Shakespeare's day had thrust stages which allowed for theater-in-the-round; the audience couldn't help but be drawn into the action. These theaters—including the Globe—Shakespeare's company was resident there—the Swan, and the Rose—were built like a "wooden O" (as Shakespeare called it). An actor could deliver a speech in a loud voice for public scenes, playing to almost all sides of the audience; in contrast, for a quiet scene such as a soliloquy, the actor could come to

right down to the edge of the stage. The stage was comparatively large, so the acoustics in these structures had to be very good for the actor to be heard in the far balconies—remember, no mikes!

Actually, the stage wasn't completely surrounded by the audience: the tiring house (where the changing rooms were) was upstage. It had an exposed second level which was used for balconies (as in *Romeo and Juliet*), and (in the case of *Julius Caesar*) for funeral orations and the rocky heights which serve as Brutus's and Cassius's lookout points during the battle. Most entrances and exits were made from upstage, through one of the two doors of the tiring-house. Since there was never much in the way of scenery or furniture, this meant that an actor coming on-stage could immediately be seen by the audience. So, in the opening speeches of some scenes, we hear dialogue that covers the time it took an actor to get to a front-and-center position. The stage was covered by an extended roof, painted to represent the heavens; it also had a trap-door in the floor which led to hell, a hiding place (where the Ghost in *Hamlet* would have been), or a dungeon.

All performances were held during the day, to make use of the natural light. In addition to the new theaters like the Globe, plays were performed at court and at trade guild-

Shakespeare Timeline

1564	William Shakespeare born to John Shakespeare and Mary Arden. He is baptized April 26.
1582	Marries Anne Hathaway in November.
1583	Daughter Susanna born, baptized May 26.
1585	Twins Hamnet and Judith born, baptized February 2.
1588-90	Sometime in these years, Shakespeare goes to London, leaving his family in Stratford. First plays performed in London.
1590-92	*The Comedy of Errors*, the three parts of *Henry VI*.
1593-94	Publication of *Venus and Adonis* and *The Rape of Lucrece*, both dedicated to the Earl of Southampton. Shakespeare becomes a shareholder in the Lord Chamberlain's Men. *The Taming of the Shrew*, *The Two Gentlemen of Verona*, *Richard III*, *Titus Andronicus*.
1595-97	*Romeo and Juliet*, *Richard II*, *King John*, *A Midsummer Night's Dream*, *Love's Labor's Lost*.
1596	Son Hamnet dies. Grant of arms to Shakespeare's father.
1597	*The Merchant of Venice*, *Henry IV, Part 1*. Purchases New Place in Stratford.
1598-1600	*Henry IV, Part 2*, *As You Like It*, *Much Ado About Nothing*, *Twelfth Night*, *The Merry Wives of Windsor*, *Henry V*, and *Julius Caesar*. Moves his company to the new Globe Theatre.
1601	*Hamlet*. Shakespeare's father dies, buried September 8.
1601-02	*Troilus and Cressida*.
1603	Death of Queen Elizabeth, succession of James VI of Scotland as James I of England. Shakespeare's company becomes The King's Men.
1603-04	*All's Well That Ends Well*, *Measure for Measure*, *Othello*.
1605-06	*King Lear*, *Macbeth*.
1607	Marriage of daughter Susanna on June 5.
1607-08	*Timon of Athens*, *Antony and Cleopatra*, *Pericles*, *Coriolanus*.
1608	Shakespeare's mother dies, buried September 9.
1609	*Cymbeline*, publication of sonnets. Shakespeare's company purchases the Blackfriars Theatre.
1610-11	*The Winter's Tale*, *The Tempest*. Shakespeare retires to Stratford.
1612-13	*Henry VIII*, *The Two Noble Kinsmen*.
1616	Marriage of daughter Judith on February 10. Shakespeare dies at Stratford on April 23.
1623	Publication of the First Folio.

halls. The costumes were in no way "realistic," as we think of the term—most of the characters wore contemporary costumes, perhaps with an element added to indicate wealth, armor, or foreign-ness. (See previous page). Thus, though no drawings remain of *Julius Caesar*, we do have one surviving from a production of *Titus Andronicus*—another of Shakespeare's "Roman" plays—and can see that the actor wore a toga-like garment over his regular costume. Of course, the biggest difference between Shakespeare's theatre and our own is that there were no female actors: all of the women's roles were played by boys—indeed, these young actors were so popular that entire theatre companies existed for them. In *Julius Caesar*, Calpurnia and Portia would have been played by such actors, and would then have served as extras in scenes where the two women weren't present.

Characters

Julius Caesar: leader of the Roman state, he has been appointed dictator-for-life by the time that the play opens. The conspirators don't object to Caesar being politically strong enough to control the lower classes—what they fear is that he might be stronger than any of *them*. As an indication of Caesar's temperament, Shakespeare has him constantly refer to himself in the third person, as if he were greater than an ordinary man. Caesar clearly feels that he is an awe-inspiring figure, but according to the play, he's infertile, partially deaf, and subject to illnesses and epileptic fits—in short, he's quite mortal. When he speaks about the dangers of which the soothsayer has warned him, Caesar says "Caesar shall forth. The things that threatened me/Ne'er looked but on my back. When they shall see/The face of Caesar, they are vanished." But Caesar is allowed only so much wisdom, and no more—the assassins' first blow comes from the back. Caesar later reappears as the Ghost, a more potent figure than his living self.

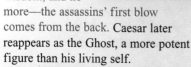

Calpurnia: *Caesar*'s wife. Calpurnia only appears in a few scenes, but her speeches help to set the play's dramatic tone by creating a feeling of tension and foreboding.

The Triumvirate

Mark Antony: Caesar's loyal follower. Antony is a soldier, but Shakespeare shows he's also a powerful speaker, able to speak persuasively when he has to. He's also not entirely honorable: he promises the mob money that Caesar had left them in his will, then cuts the bequest. When he, Octavius and Lepidus meet to decide what action to take in this, the newest round of civil wars, Antony calmly agrees to his own nephew's death. Perhaps Antony recognizes his own double-standards,

and blames the conspirators for not recognizing their own, for committing murder in the name of lofty (but hypocritical) ideals. At the end of the play, Antony praises Brutus as the only one of the conspirators with pure motives. No matter what his faults, though, it's clear that Antony truly loved, and truly grieves for, Caesar; this relationship is one of the several father-son prototypes that Shakespeare offers in the play.

Octavius: in real life, Caesar's great-nephew, and in the play, clearly another son-like figure to the great Julius. He's more like Cassius than like Antony, his supposed ally. Shakespeare more fully develops Octavius in his later tragedy *Antony and Cleopatra*, but we see hints here of a steely young man who will take orders from no one, not even Antony:

Antony	Octavius, lead your battle softly on Upon the left hand of the even field.
Octavius	Upon the right hand I. Keep thou the left.
Antony	Why do you cross me in this exigent?
Octavius	I do not cross you; but I will do so.

Octavius is a man who knows what he wants, and for all of Antony's powers of persuasion, he's helpless before Octavius's unwielding stubbornness.

Lepidus: is in only one scene, which shows the triumvirate coldly planning to consolidate their hold over Rome. Antony discounts Lepidus as no more important than a war-horse that knows how to take orders. In fact, we don't even see Lepidus as a "war-horse:" he doesn't appear in the battle scenes. Dramatically, the conflict between Antony and Octavius is more interesting (and ultimately more important) than anything Lepidus is involved in.

The Soothsayer: tries to warn Caesar that the Ides (15th) of March will be a dangerous day for him. In fact, Caesar is assassinated on just that day. The soothsayer makes two appearances, once in the first scene (a month or so prior to the assassination in "real time") and once just before the murder. As he goes to the Capitol in the company of the conspirators, Caesar notes "The Ides of March art come," to which the Soothsayer wisely replies "Aye, Caesar, but not gone."

Flavius and Marullus: Roman tribunes. They set the play's mood of tension and strife in the very first scene, showing that Caesar, celebrating his triumph over Pompey, isn't popular with everyone. The two tribunes are disgusted by the mob's fickle spirit, and talk disparagingly about the common people. We don't see these two again after this opening scene, and Casca later reports that they were "put to silence for pulling scarves off Caesar's images," a fact that fuels the conspirators' resentment against Caesar.

The Mob: Roman citizenry is presented in the very first scene as an actor in the play; some are individually identified (First Plebeian, Second Plebeian, etc.—a plebeian is a commoner), but for the most part they speak with one voice. How the mob's point-of-view may change under the influence of an impassioned speech is one of the themes of the play. Many scholars have debated how little or how much respect Shakespeare had for the mob—are they true foes of tyranny, or are they slavish followers of the most persuasive politician?

The Conspirators:

MY ANCESTORS DID, FROM THE STREETS OF ROME, THE TARQUIN DRIVE WHEN HE WAS CALLED A KING. AM I ENTREATED TO SPEAK AND STRIKE?... SOMEONE KNOCKS!

Brutus: a descendent of the legendary Lucius Junius Brutus, who drove out the last kings from Rome centuries before the action of this play and who went on to found the Republic. This Brutus is bound by nostalgia for the "good old days" of the Republic, but the days he longs for never really existed, and it is Brutus's tragic flaw that he can't distinguish between political nostalgia and reality. This leads to a tension between what he is and what he does:

Brutus constantly speaks of honor, but do his actions support this ideal? He murders his close friend (and father-figure—it's even said that Brutus might be Caesar's illegitimate son) and causes a brutal civil war in which honor is *dis*honored—all for the sake of an idealized, romanticized Rome. Brutus's idea of honor and loyalty is sincere, but it's too easy for him to rationalize his way out of honorable and loyal behavior. Like Hamlet, another of Shakespeare's great introspective characters, he's trying to arrive at self-understanding; unlike Hamlet, he never achieves it. Brutus does know that what he's plotting is bad: it keeps him awake at night. And on the eve of battle, when Brutus encounters the Ghost of Caesar, the apparition tells Brutus it represents his own evil spirit—in modern terms, his bad conscience. Brutus is a Stoic, which means that he cannot allow himself "vexed passions:" a Stoic never shows emotion over personal issues, even over the death of his wife. As he says of himself, "No man bears sorrow better."

Cassius: Caesar voices his dislike and suspicion of Cassius in one of Shakespeare's most famous lines: "Yon Cassius has a lean and hungry look; he thinks too much; such men are dangerous." In this, Cassius is unlike Antony, who loves plays and music. Cassius's motive in murdering Caesar seems to be jealousy; however, we can't say that Cassius is all bad. Consider how Cassius appears at the end of the play: though Brutus accuses him of corruption, and Cassius never fully explains away the charge, Cassius maintains that his own personal code of honor is as worthy as Brutus's. His respect for Brutus is obvious, and his sorrow over the news of Portia's death is real. In addition, Cassius's own men honor him and willingly die with him. Despite his guilt, Cassius is at least true to himself: when he calls Antony "a masker and a reveller," Antony, noting Cassius's constancy, comes back with "Old Cassius still."

Casca: Cassius notes that Casca speaks in a "sour fashion," and indeed he's a grim person. Not only does Casca despise Caesar for his epilepsy, he also mocks the mob in telling how they responded to Antony's offer of the crown to Caesar: "...and still as he (Caesar) refused it the rabblement hooted and clapped their chapped hands and threw up their sweaty nightcaps and uttered such a deal of stinking breath because Caesar refused the crown that it had almost choked Caesar...for

I FEAR HIM NOT: YET, IF MY NAME WERE LIABLE TO FEAR, I DO NOT KNOW THE MAN I SHOULD AVOID SO SOON AS THAT SPARE CASSIUS. HE LOVES NO PLAYS. SELDOM DOES HE SMILE. SUCH MEN AS HE BE NEVER AT HEART'S EASE... I RATHER TELL THEE WHAT IS TO BE FEARED THAN WHAT I FEAR; FOR ALWAYS I AM CAESAR.

mine own part, I durst not laugh for fear of opening my lips and receiving the bad air." Such a man wouldn't advocate popular freedom, only liberty for the aristocracy and upper classes.

Decius Brutus: although he only appears in the first part of the play, Decius Brutus is vital to the events that unfold. He's the one who makes sure that Caesar goes to the Capitol on the Ides of March; Decius's powers of persuasion prove he's a consummate politician. Decius knows Caesar's character well, saying he can persuade Caesar to do anything because "I tell him he hates flatterers...(and Caesar is) then most flattered." When Caesar tells him about Calpurnia's dream, Decius answers "This dream is all amiss interpreted," and from that moment on, Caesar's fate is sealed.

Cinna: known as **Cinna the Conspirator**, he plays a role in the initial plotting and in the murder, but isn't seen after that. We should not, as the mob does, confuse him with *Cinna the Poet*: in the play, the Poet is murdered simply because he bears the same name as the conspirator. Even when he protests that he's a *different* Cinna, a poet and not a conspirator, the blood-thirsty crowd finds a reason in this to murder him, as they shout "Tear him for his bad verses, tear him for his bad verses!"

Portia: Brutus's wife, she demands to know what's bothering her husband, saying that she should be able to help him in all things. In the spirit of his own time as well as of ancient Rome, in Brutus's responses Shakespeare questions whether a woman can hold her tongue, even whether she'd be capable of giving useful advice to a man. Portia appears only once more after that; later Brutus tells Cassius that, despairing over his absence and the civil war, she has swallowed "fire" (live coals) and so committed suicide.

The Plot

Julius Caesar takes its cue from Shakespeare's history plays, written in the decade preceding its premiere; but it's more than just a chronicle play. *Julius Caesar* is a tragedy, and was to be followed by *Hamlet* and a string of other great tragedies. But unlike *Hamlet*, *Julius Caesar*'s tragedy is not relieved by much humor. There is no sense of rejoicing at the play's end for justice achieved; there is only relief that civil war is over and civil order restored. Apart from a few ironic and sardonic asides, there is little attempt to break up the cynical atmosphere born of dangerous politicking. *Julius Caesar* was a success in its day, and continues to be one of Shakespeare's more popular plays, both for study and performance. It was first published in 1623 in the First Folio, a collection of Shakespeare's plays put out by John Heminge and Henry Condell, who'd been actors in Shakespeare's company.

Julius Caesar opens at a point in history when Rome had undergone nearly a century of brutal civil wars. The Republic to which Brutus and Cassius refer with fatal nostalgia throughout the play had never functioned as a true democracy (it was a democracy only for Roman men—women and slaves didn't count). The Republic itself had become a political football, with political and military strongmen kicking it back and forth in the struggle for power. Just before the play begins, Caesar has conquered Pompey, the previous strongman. An ancient Roman festival, the Lupercalia, is being celebrated, and Caesar has turned the day into a political holiday celebrating his victory over Pompey. Two tribunes, enraged that he has done so, angrily tell some workers celebrating in the streets that Caesar is wrong, and the tribunes decide to tear down all the decorations for Caesar's triumph. Then Caesar enters, accompanied by his wife Calpurnia, his trusted friend Mark Antony, and a host of Roman dignitaries. After Caesar leaves with his retinue, Brutus and Cassius remain to discuss the new political situation in Rome.

It quickly becomes clear that Cassius dislikes Caesar. He tells of a time he and Caesar swam the River Tiber and Caesar almost drowned, and expresses his frustration at the thought that any man, especially one whom *he* saved from drowning, should try to establish himself as a god over other men. Brutus too fears that Caesar is trying to become a king, and maybe even a god; this fear is confirmed when Casca returns to say that Antony has just offered Caesar the crown three times. Brutus, extremely troubled, leaves, and Cassius notes that Brutus may now be ripe to join a conspiracy to kill Caesar.

Shakespeare now condenses real time—the month between the

Lupercalia and the Ides of March— for dramatic effect; the story shifts to the night before the assassination: on the street, Casca meets Cicero. It's a stormy night, and Casca tells of many strange and horrible sights in Rome: wild animals roaming the streets and flames shooting from the bodies of men. Despite these omens, Cassius joins Casca, and they resolve to murder Caesar. They agree that they need Brutus on their side to get public acceptance of their deed.

Next, we see that Brutus too is awake, wandering restlessly in his orchard, debating what to do about Caesar. The conspirators come as a group to his house, and there they all commit to the scheme to murder Caesar. Brutus forbids the murder of anyone but Caesar, because that would seem like butchery. When the conspirators want to swear an oath to solidify their bond, Brutus forbids this as well: for Brutus, the fact that they are Romans is enough to seal the agreement. Portia, Brutus's wife, joins him after the others leave, but he won't tell her what has happened.

Caesar and Calpurnia, too, aren't getting much rest on this disturbed night. She warns Caesar not to go to the Capitol the next day, the Ides of March, but every reason she gives for him *not* to go is craftily countered by Decius Brutus, who comes near dawn, expressly to persuade Caesar to go to the Capitol. He deliberately mistranslates Calpurnia's images of murder and death into scenes of honor and glory for Caesar; Decius Brutus outtalks Calpurnia, and so leads Caesar to his death. Antony, just before the murder, is tricked by one of the conspirators into leaving Caesar's side, so that he can't prevent the assassination.

TOTTERING, CAESAR TURNED TO BRUTUS FOR ASSISTANCE, BUT AVOIDING HIS FACE, BRUTUS, TOO, WIELDED HIS SWORD...

Then, in a famously bloody and horrific scene, Caesar is killed. We watch as Brutus tries to rationalize the murder, making it into something like a religious ritual; he continually refers to the murder as a sacrifice, and has the murderers wash their hands in Caesar's blood, as if to justify the righteousness of the action. Caesar is dead when Antony returns, and he tells the murderers that he's sure they had their reasons for what they did, and that if they want to kill him too, he can think of no better time, no better place to die than with Julius Caesar. Cassius would be happy to oblige, but Brutus not only overrules Cassius by welcoming Antony, but permits the secretly-outraged Antony to give the last part of Caesar's funeral oration. As Cassius under-

stands, the last person to speak in a debate usually has the advantage: by letting Antony speak last, Brutus has done himself and his fellow conspirators a fatal disservice.

What follows is one of the most famous scenes in Shakespeare: first Brutus, then Antony, gives a speech over Caesar's body, before the Roman citizenry. Brutus convinces the crowd that the murder was justified; Antony convinces them it was not. By using sarcasm, Antony is able to take every statement Brutus has made and turn it on its head. Shakespeare's genius lies in presenting two utterly logical speeches—one right after the other—that so completely contradict each other, nothing short of a civil war can come from it. In Antony's famous opening lines we can hear how he immediately joins issues of personal sorrow with matters of state:

Friends, Romans, countrymen, lend me your ears;
I come to bury Caesar, not to praise him.
The evil that men do lives after them;
The good is oft interred with their bones.

In the wake of the riots that follow his speech, Antony joins forces with Octavius and Lepidus. The civil war that follows the assassination is worse than what might have happened had Julius Caesar been made king. Cassius and Brutus continue as friends—the other conspirators have dropped out of the picture by now—though they argue before the battle over accusations of Cassius's dishonesty. When they reconcile, Brutus tells Cassius that Portia is dead; Cassius is pained for his friend. They agree they will never let themselves be taken alive, to be paraded as captives through the streets of Rome. Brutus is visited by the Ghost of Caesar, which tells him they shall meet again at Philippi. Finally, at Phillipi, Antony and Octavius defeat Cassius and Brutus, and we witness Brutus's suicide. Antony pays tribute to Brutus at the end, saying "This was the noblest Roman of them all."

CAESAR, NOW BE STILL. I KILL'D NOT THEE WITH HALF SO GOOD A WILL..

syllable followed by a stressed syllable (da **dum**, da **dum**, da **dum**, da **dum**, da **dum**). An example of this is the last two lines of the play, where Octavius says "So **call** the **field** to **rest**, and **let's a**way/To **part** the **glories of** this **happy day**." The pattern of iambic pentameter is very similar to the basic rhythms of spoken English. Sometimes these verse lines rhyme, but often they do not; this is called "blank verse." Though the lines may look like poetry, when they are spoken, they sound natural and unforced. The CI adaptation puts many of the verse speeches into prose form, but we can still get a sense of their poetry when we read the lines out loud.

A standard practice in Elizabethan drama was to assign verse to the nobility or to lovers, and prose to commoners or to someone of a very down-to-earth nature, but this practice too was altered create an effect. For instance, a character who is normally very practical might express his thoughts on love in verse. On the other hand, a nobleman who is expressing distinctly ignoble thoughts might speak in prose. How Shakespeare uses verse and prose is a clue to the mood of the scene; it may be an indication of what he thinks of that character in that given moment. In *Julius Caesar*, when Casca meets Brutus and Cassius and

Poetry and Structure

How does Shakespeare make this story work in dramatic terms? Fundamentally, his dramaturgy (how the play functions as a piece of dramatic writing) has two building blocks: language and scene structure. Shakespeare wrote in "iambic pentameter," a verse form in which each line of verse is broken into five sections per line. The sections are called feet, and "iamb" refers to the pattern of stress in the foot: a light

describes how Mark Antony offered the crown to Caesar, the text is in prose; usually a patrician like Casca would speak in verse. Was Shakespeare trying to indicate something about the nobility, or lack thereof, in Casca's character? Then, in the next scene, Casca meets Cicero in the dark, stormy night, and the talk is of omens, portents, and unnatural phenomena; here Casca speaks in verse, the better to create atmosphere and a sense of dread in the audience.

Shakespeare's language catches our attention in other ways: he frequently invented new words, based on accepted forms (such as Lady Macbeth's famous plea to the spirits to "unsex" her). This subversion of a single word could be matched by the way Shakespeare subverted sentence structure, playing on accepted word definition and function, turning words and phrases on their heads, using them in meanings distinct from their original one. For instance, Cassius speaks of "weeping his spirit" through his eyes; an unusual, grabby image. Shakespeare also uses repetition to enhance a scene's mood: after the assassination, Brutus says "Stoop, Romans, stoop/And let us bathe our hands in Caesar's blood," and Cassius continues with "Stoop then and wash." The language suggests a religious rite, which is just what Brutus thinks the event

Superstition

O that a man might know the end of this day's business ere it come!

In ancient Rome, people believed they could foretell the future by a number of methods, ways we no longer credit (much), including astrology, divination, prophecy, and animal sacrifice. The second scene of the play demonstrates this, as the Soothsayer calls out to Caesar "Beware the Ides of March!" Romans also read meaning into phenomena of nature like thunder-storms and animals behaving strangely. In Shakespeare's day, more than 1500 years after the time of *Julius Caesar*, people still believed in the power of evil spirits, and that one person could use these evil spirits to put a curse on someone else. As a safeguard against such threats, astrology and other means of predicting and forecasting the future were used in the hopes that the universe could be made more familiar and manageable. King James I of England, Elizabeth I's successor, was afraid of, yet intrigued by, witches; it's believed that Shakespeare included witches in his play *Macbeth* specifically for the king's entertainment. In *Hamlet*, the play written just after *Julius*

WHAT SAY THE AUGERERS?'

THEY WOULD NOT HAVE YOU STIR FORTH TODAY. PLUCKING THE ENTRAILS OF AN OFFERING, THEY COULD NOT FIND A HEART WITHIN THE BEAST.

'ROMAN PROPHETS

should be. Antony, later in the scene, carefully shakes the bloody hand of each conspirator, naming each as he goes along. This listing of the names adds a note of solemnity, while it also lends his speech a subtly threatening tone.

There's a very spare and careful use of the soliloquy in this play. These solo speeches are used for a number of different reasons: they can define a character and reveal motives, as Antony does after the conspirators leave him with Caesar's body; they can

WOE TO THE HAND THAT SHED THIS COSTLY BLOOD, FOR CAESAR'S SPIRIT, RANGING FOR REVENGE, SHALL IN THESE CONFINES CRY HAVOC! THIS FOUL DEED SHALL SMELL ABOVE THE EARTH.

highlight themes of the play, as when Brutus ponders why Caesar should or should not die; and, theatrically they create a bond between the actor and audience.

The structure of *Julius Caesar* also helps us understand its plot and themes. The play is presented mainly in a succession of short scenes, which give a sense of constant motion and allows the audience to see the essence of action. For example, at the very end of the play there's a series of battles: obviously,

Caesar, Shakespeare again uses a ghostly figure as a character to great effect; he also has Hamlet tell a friend "There are more things in heaven and earth, Horatio, than are dreamt of in your philosophy." And in *Julius Caesar*, Cassius serves to check this mood, when he says,

Men at some time are masters of their fates.

The fault, dear Brutus, is not in our stars,

But in ourselves...

Before we condemn the Romans (and Elizabethans) for naiveté, remember that even today, stormy weather in horror movies usually indicates something (or someone) scary is about to come into the picture; you can see how belief in the supernatural lingers with us yet.

It's very difficult for a writer to take a story with a well-known ending and make it fresh and interesting again.

Shakespeare was able to do it in part because of the dramatic tension he creates by using supernatural elements. Much of the talk of omens and harbingers of doom come early on in the play, and it establishes a mood of tension and suspense. Much of his audience probably knew Caesar's story, and they also probably knew the outcome of the ensuing Battle of Philippi. In order to sell tickets to his play, and to keep people watching the play, Shakespeare had to provide the audience with something new in terms of how the story progressed. By playing on his audience's fascination with the supernatural, Shakespeare wrote a play that worked in re-creating a moment in history so that it became immediately accessible and meaningful for that audience. Almost 400 years later the play, through such devices, still works.

no stage production can realistically show a full battle. Shakespeare solved this dilemma by having certain characters act as eyes for other characters, and thus for the audience. What we are allowed to see and know, and when we are allowed this vision and knowledge, is as carefully controlled as anything a filmmaker would show us through the camera lens. For example, when Cassius has Pindarus watch Titinius's progress, we hear, along with Cassius, a false report of Titinius's capture. But what we see that Cassius does *not* is that Titinius was met by friendly forces; Cassius, dead at Pindarus's hand, will never know it.

While shifts in place and time within the play can be immediate and drastic, the audience accepts it because the language, the dialogue, sets the scene. Often the dialogue of one character serves to announce the entrance of another character: Brutus says "The games are done, and Caesar is returning." The Greek and Roman drama the Elizabethans admired required "unity of time and place"—that is, that plays should take place in the same time-frame, and in the same location. But Shakespeare, like his contemporaries, was trying for something else. What they were reaching for, and what Shakespeare succeeded in brilliantly, was creating *atmospheric* unity.

Shakespeare's plays have a built-in theatricality to them, and include not just cues to the actor, hidden in the text, but references to theater, plays, and playing that the audience would appreciate. In *Hamlet,* the actor playing old Polonius probably got quite a laugh when the character says he'd once played Caesar and was killed in the Capitol—since it's possible that the actor really had played Caesar in the Roman play a few years earlier. The audience itself was the butt of an insult from Casca's lips, when he speaks of Caesar: "If the rag-tag people did not clap him and hiss him, according as he pleased and displeased him them, as they do the players in the theatre, I am no true man." Of course, the irony here is that Casca *isn't* a "true man:" whoever says those lines is one of those 'players in the theatre.'

Some of the hidden directions in the text are stage directions. Cassius tells Brutus to "pluck Casca by the sleeve," and we can assume the actor playing Brutus does just this when Casca passes by, for Casca says "You pulled me by the cloak." Later, just before the murder, there is no indication that Decius Brutus must kneel in front of Caesar, but when Caesar asks "Doth not Brutus bootless kneel?" we can be pretty sure that the actor playing Decius has done just that. 'Bootless', incidentally, doesn't mean that Decius was barefoot; it means to do something without hope of success. It's part of the fun of rehearsal for actors to find these directions out as they go through the script. In one production a director, seeing that there was no stage direction given to disperse the murderers, had his Cassius step right over Caesar's corpse as a way of emphasizing Cassius's disdain for the dead man. Shakespeare, the consummate man of the theatre, knew these discoveries could be worked out in each production, and that they would add to depth of each performance.

Themes

THE THEATER OF POLITICS: *All the world's a stage/And all the men and women merely players...* These lines are from Shakespeare's comedy *As You Like It,* but they resonate in *Julius Caesar* as well. The lines from the earlier comedy seem to flow into the passage from this tragedy, in Cassius's musing "How many ages hence/Shall this our lofty scene be acted over/In states unborn and accents yet unknown!" So says Cassius as he contemplates the bloody, lifeless form of Caesar. It's no accident that Shakespeare draws our attention to the theatricality of this moment. *Julius Caesar* is a play which examines, among other things, the *staging* of politics. Statesmen play at being patriots, patriots play at being soothsayers, and the drama plays at being historical fact. Both Brutus and Antony understand the importance of explaining their point-of-view to the Roman populace; the fact that Antony is the more self-conscious of the two—that he's the one playing a role—as he gives his speech, is one of the reasons his oration is more successful politically than was Brutus's. Rhetoric is shown here to be a powerful political tool. Another theatrical theme is the treatment of the characters' tendency to 'cast' themselves in roles for which they are ill-suited. Caesar sees himself as an indestructible force, though the fact that he suffers from certain infirmities should be sufficient to warn him of his vulnerability. He refuses to admit doubt, thinking that would suggest weakness on his part. Soon, though, it appears that Caesar did not study his part well enough: shortly after telling the conspirators "I am as constant as the Northern Star," he gasps out "Then fall Caesar" as he dies.

POLITICS OR PEOPLE: *Not that I loved Caesar less, but that I loved Rome more...*

The play asks which is more important, the individual or the state? How do we make such decisions— are we truly free to do so? Do people define politics, or does politics define people? Even if we have honorable motives for our actions, can we be sure that our actions will remain true to their intentions? Brutus thinks his character and his beliefs are what distinguish this conspiracy from ordinary murder, yet his actions precipitate a ruthless civil war that will begin (See next page) Rome's new life as an empire—the

THEN NONE I OFFENDED. HERE COMES CAESAR'S BODY, MOURNED BY MARK ANTONY, WHO HAD NO PART IN HIS DEATH. WITH THIS I SLEW MY BEST LOVER FOR THE GOOD OF ROME. I HAVE THE SAME DAGGER FOR MYSELF WHEN IT SHALL PLEASE MY COUNTRY TO NEED MY DEATH.

very thing Brutus suspected Julius Caesar of wanting. We will never know if that in fact is what Caesar would have done; Brutus and the other conspirators tried to prevent fate from taking its course, and instead helped it on its way. Antony predicts "Domestic fury and fierce civil strife/Shall cumber all the parts of Italy," and he's proven correct. Brutus, Cassius, and their allies try to control the political destiny of Rome, and instead find it controlling them.

WHAT IS A HERO? *Am I entreated to speak and strike?*

What defines a hero? Is it someone who answers the call of conscience, or of country? In *Julius Caesar*, it isn't clear who the hero is—is it the title character? (Hamlet is, after all, the hero of *Hamlet*.) Is it Brutus, whose character seems to draw the main focus—but who murders his nation's leader, his own friend? How can this be considered heroic? Is it Antony, who proves his loyalty to his leader—but also cheats the populace of their inheritance from Caesar? Most critics agree

Brutus has as much right as any of the characters to be called the 'hero' of the piece, but we can see how Brutus's actions could be considered traitorous. There are no easy definitions of the word 'hero' in this play, and hence no easy identification of who its hero might be.

THE FATHER-FIGURE: *the most unkindest cut of all...*

This plays examines several different father-son relationships—we have noted already that Caesar is like a father to Antony, Brutus, and Octavius (though in different respects to each man). We can also look at Caesar as the political "father" of Rome. But what does such a phrase mean? That we owe a political leader respect in the same way that we owe it to a parent? Antony's rage comes partly from the fact that Brutus had been like a son to Caesar—he says Brutus had been "Caesar's angel"—and it's this "ingratitude" which killed Caesar, Antony says, as much as any of the blows from the knife (See next Page).

NATIONAL IDENTITY: *A son of Rome...*

People in this play are constantly talking about what defines a 'true' Roman. They use these definitions as a spur and justification to action. Cassius says "Rome, thou hast lost the breed of noble bloods," and convinces Brutus that his identity as a 'true' Roman is in question; because of this subtle threat, Brutus begins to favor the conspiracy. In Shakespeare's time, England was coming into its own as a political power; questions of national identity were becoming of primary concern to late 16th century Europe, and England was no exception. In Shakespeare's *Henry V*, one soldier from each of the different countries of the British Isles—Ireland, England, Scotland, and Wales—argues the merits of their own country, but the fact remains that they are all in a common trench, waiting to fight a common enemy. This is as true a definition of nationhood as any. But *Julius Caesar* turns the question into material for tragedy; in defending the name of 'Roman,' many Romans are killed. Civil wars, it's said, threaten a nation's identity more thoroughly than any other kind of war. Which might be called the 'truer' Roman, someone from Octavius and Antony's faction or someone from Cassius and Brutus's faction?

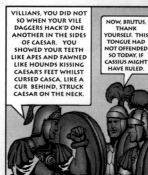

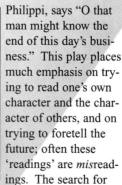

SELF-KNOWLEDGE: *the eye sees not itself...*

Brutus, before the Battle of Philippi, says "O that man might know the end of this day's business." This play places much emphasis on trying to read one's own character and the character of others, and on trying to foretell the future; often these 'readings' are *mis*readings. The search for clarity of vision is played out both in literary terms and in physical terms. In Cassius's and Brutus's first meeting, Brutus tells Cassius that he has lately been concerned with some issues which he has kept private. Cassius, already alert to the possibility of playing Brutus for the purposes of the conspiracy, asks "Tell me good Brutus, can you see your face?" Brutus responds "No Cassius, for the eye sees not itself/But by reflection, by some other things." This is all Cassius needs: he presents himself as the "mirror" with which Brutus may truly see himself. In this situation, Cassius has the sharper vision because he knows himself well; Brutus, who doubts himself, is persuaded to see himself through another's eyes.

•In recent years there have been a number of filmed versions of Shakespeare's plays, including *Romeo and Juliet*, *Othello*, *Much Ado About Nothing*, and two *Hamlets*. Why are these stories of interest today? Julius Caesar covers issues of politics, honor, and self-knowledge; how do these issues relate to our own lives? How can a playwright who lived four hundred years ago speak to our concerns today?

•Do you think Shakespeare wants the audience to take the power of the supernatural seriously in this play? Remember, Calpurnia's dreams truthfully predict what will happen on the Ides of March—why does Shakespeare take so much care to establish the fact that this vision, and the appearance of Caesar's ghost, are trustworthy omens?

•What do you think of Cassius: are his actions motivated by personal jealousy only, or does he act out of concern for Rome? Remember, though Antony offers the final word on the conspirators at the play's end, his judgment of Cassius could be tainted by their mutual dislike.

•Has the definition of the words "patriot" and "hero" changed over time? What did they mean in Caesar's day? In Shakespeare's? In our own? Can people ignore the law when they feel they are morally justified in their action? Consider the conspirators in *Julius Caesar*, the people involved in the civil rights movement of the 1960s, and the various players in Watergate. How might the terms 'patriot' and 'hero' be applied, or not, to these people.

•Look over Antony's funeral oration. What tools does he use to stir the mob to anger? What references does he make to Brutus's speech, and how does he manipulate them? What do you think Shakespeare is saying about the power of persuasive speech?

•When watching *Julius Caesar*, what effect on a speech would an intensely poetic sound have? Can you find examples in a script of *Julius Caesar* where Shakespeare uses rhymed iambic pentameter? unrhymed? another verse form altogether?

•Consider some of the choices you might make as a director of Julius Caesar. Would you use Roman dress, Elizabethan dress, modern dress or a mixture of all three? Would you use all male actors, as Shakespeare did (and what would this choice mean to a modern audience)? Some directors place the actors playing members of the mob among the audience; would you? What effect might this choice have on an audience member sitting next to one of the actors?

About the Essayist:

Julie Bleha is a dramaturge, and an Instructor at Columbia University, where she is also a President's Fellow and a doctoral candidate. She holds an M.A. in drama from King's College, London.